Contents

Mark Reid art.com

Fantasy Cats

Introduction

ILLUSION

Since the launch of *Illusion* in 2006, New Mexico-born Mark Reid has been a good friend to us. We featured him in the very first issue of the magazine, when he admitted to our readers that he even paints in his sleep!

At the tender age of five, Mark decided he would be an artist for the rest of his life. After graduating from Colorado Institute of Art he made a living from his fine art, graphic design and murals. He started face painting at small festivals, as a hobby, in 1994. It was not until 2002, when he experienced a 'eureka' moment on viewing his first face-painted tiger (see p5), that he switched direction to become a full-time face and body painter.

Since then Mark has gone from strength to strength and is now a prominent and much-loved figure within the international face and body painting community. He spends his time traveling the world painting, competing and teaching. He won sixth and third place respectively in the brush and sponge competitions at the 2007 and 2008 World Bodypainting Festival held in Seeboden, Austria.

Mark is perhaps best known for his instantly recognisable wildcat faces, so we were delighted when he agreed to publish this book with us and share some of his secrets. In this book he has specially created 12 new cat faces for you to try. But these step-by-steps are just a starting point. We hope you will use Mark's style and technical tips and adapt his ideas to create your own endless possibilities.

Happy painting.

Claire and Julie

My First Tiger

The first tiger face I saw changed my life forever. This may sound a little melodramatic, but it's true.

It was back in 2002. I was setting up for a festival in Grapevine, Texas, when an elderly lady approached me and asked for work. She pulled out a small photo album and showed me the said life-changing tiger face. I had a flashback to the day when, aged five, I stood transfixed watching a man painting a mural. I literally lost my breath.

At that time, I had been doing cheek art for some eight years, two or three times a year, using acrylic paint. I didn't know that professional face make-up existed.

I said: "Can you teach me to do that?"

"Yes of course," she replied. "Get your stuff."

The wonderful tiger woman was Judy Kubrik. In the picture the tiger on the left is mine and the one on the right is hers. I tried to copy Judy step-by-step. Never once did I think I would now be doing this for a living – not only this, but painting, competing and teaching face and body art all over the world. And it all started with this tiger.

Rest in peace, Judy, and thank you so much for finding me.

It took me 20 minutes to do this first tiger. I couldn't handle the sponges and I was at a loss trying to figure out where to put the lines and how to make them work. However, I became determined to cut the time it took to at least half.

I copied Judy. I copied Olivier Ziegers. I copied Jinny. I mixed them together. And I figured it out. I found the secret to the three-minute tiger and I learnt how to create a new design every time without sacrificing quality or quantity.

Now, I want to share some of this experience and knowledge with you.

The designs in this book were created on the spur of the moment without planning. Being able to produce designs by request, without hesitation, is the key to endless possibilities. I think we face painters are like Columbus, with each child's face as the world waiting to be discovered. I cannot stress enough the importance of smooth blending and clean flawless lines. Also, if you pay attention to the flow and balance of your design and remember to use the focal point, your designs will reach a new level.

I hope this book will instruct and inspire you.

Mark
www.markreidart.com

Blending and Brush Techniques

Equipment

Choosing the right sponges and brushes is very much a case of finding the ones that feel right for you. This may involve quite a bit of trial and error. Personally, as you will see in the following step-by-step designs, I only use two different brushes: a number four for my line work and a number three for details. I still like to try new number four brushes once in a while though.

After trying numerous sponges, I came across one that really suited me – it is the best sponge I have used. It's very durable and long lasting and lets me apply a nice base very easily. It's also great for 'dabbing' and doesn't seem to stain.

You can see you don't need much to create fabulous cat faces. The only other piece of equipment I use to produce the following designs is a large smoothie blender for applying gem powders.

Loading the Sponge

Use a water mister to spray the surface of the cake. Drag the sponge across with minimal pressure several times until the cake is dry again.

Apply make-up to the face, again with minimal pressure. If the sponge is too wet, there will be streaks. Pat the sponge on a dry towel to remove any excess moisture.

Be sure to apply under the eyes with the edge of the sponge while the model looks up.

Apply colours randomly for your design, softly stroking the sponge into the first colour to create an airbrushed look.

Perfect Lines

Creating perfect lines is much easier than you might think. Loading the brush with paint properly and paying attention to the tip of your brush can help you to achieve this. As I said above, I like to use a number four round brush for my line work.

When you load your brush, dip it in water once or mist the surface of the cake by spraying it once. Pull the brush back at a 45 degree angle. Turn it over and do it again several times to make sure the make-up and water are well mixed. Do not move the brush in a sideways motion as it will damage the bristles.

When you are finished, your bristles should look FAT and FLAT.

Airplane Landing, Airplane Taking Off...

When I start a line, I like to think of it as an airplane landing on a runway. The flat bristles should approach the skin like a knife about to cut a steak. As you pull the brush, flatten the bristles about half way down and slightly roll the brush between your fingers. As you watch the tip of the brush, start to raise it gradually so as to create the effect of an airplane taking off.

You MUST pay attention to the tip of the brush, so that you will know when to raise it from the surface as it creates a point. Always follow through with your stroke.

Every Step I Take...

This set of detailed photographs show exactly how I hold the sponge and make each brush stroke, for you to refer to until you are confidently creating your very own signature tigers.

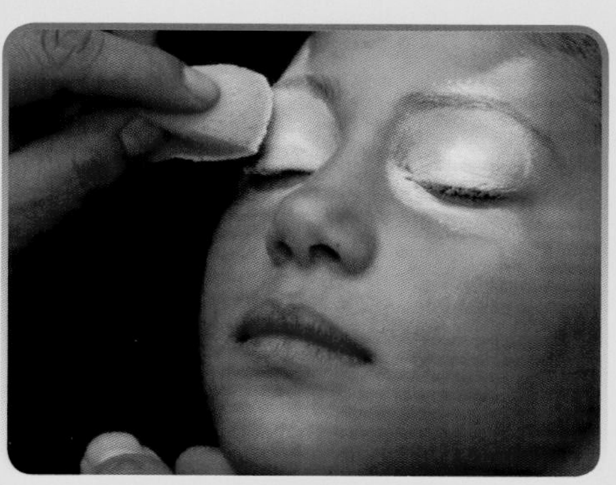

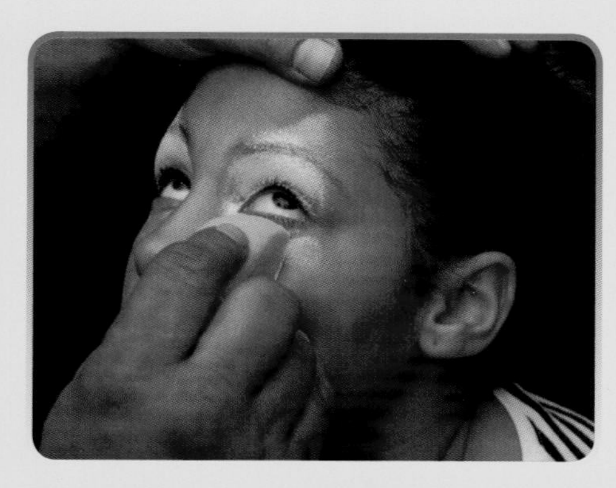

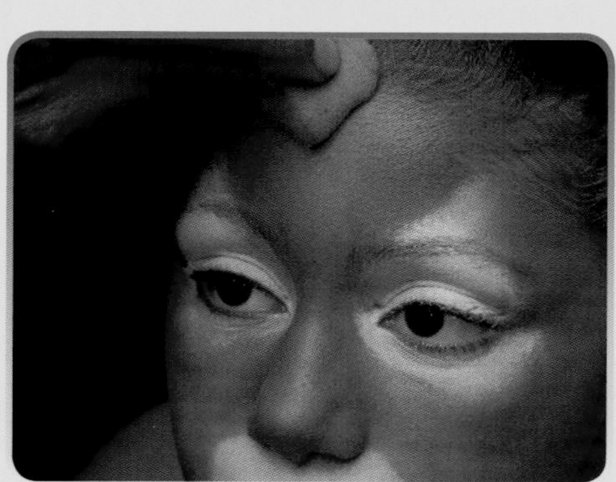

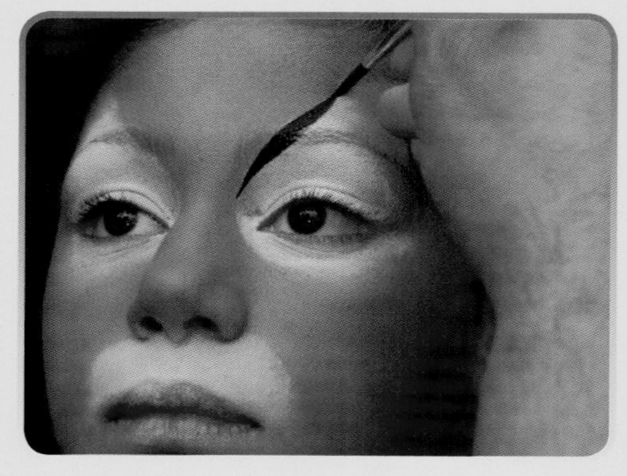

Basic Spotted Cat

Cheetah, leopard, call it what you will – this design doubles for both. Use simple dots or, as I have here, a tiger line with a 'u-turn' in it.

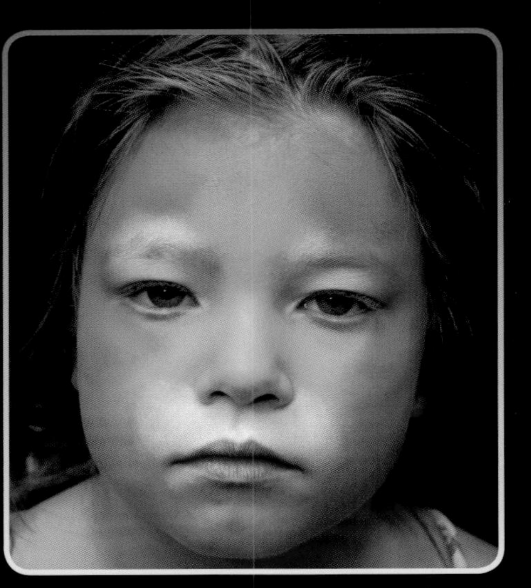

1 Sponge on a base. Here, I use white for the muzzle and eyes, lime for the nose and teal to define the shape of the face on the forehead and cheekbones.

2 Use black to line the eyelids and cat eyebrows.

3 Next u-turns! Start with an upward stroke then lay the bristles down halfway to the ferrule, then bring the brush back down to end in a point. Paint these markings in black on the forehead between the brows. Make sure they start small in the centre and get larger as they near the hairline.

4 Continue with more u-turns across the cheeks. Paint the lips red and then outline in black. Finish by painting a black nose

A basic tiger for beginners – three colours and minimal stripes. It is effective for lines of queuing customers as, with practice, it can be done in two and a half minutes.

1 As with the Basic Spotted Cat, sponge on the base in three colours. I use white for the muzzle and eyes, mango between the eyes and over the nose, and orange to shape the face around the cheeks and forehead.

2 With a number four round brush, thickly line the eyes in black to a point at the outside corners.

3 Add black stripes to the forehead, radiating from the focal point right between the eyes. Continue using black

4 Add cheek lines, again flowing from the focal point. Line the lips in black and fill with red and add glitter.

Model: Tommi Olivia

5 Use lines of dots to create whisker holes. By paying attention to the flow of the lines in this design you will be adding your own lines to create your own signature tiger in no time at all.

Abstract Cat

This cat forms a pair with Rainbow Cat. Focused on opposite sides of the face, these designs look particularly good when photographed together.

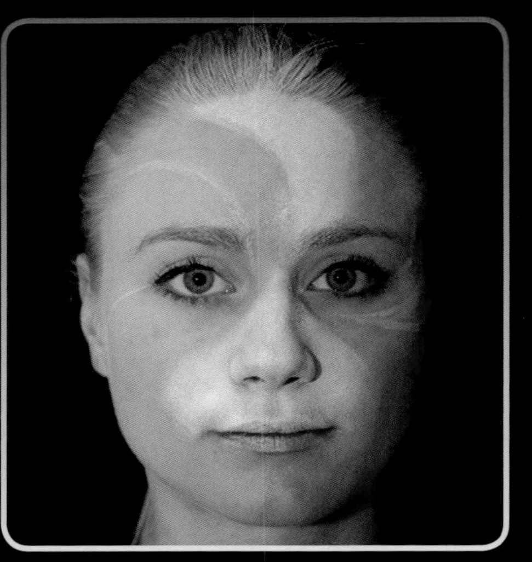

1 Using a large smoothie blender, paint a white muzzle. Continue over the nose and up the forehead to create a strong swirl design.

2 Still using the smoothie blender, apply gem powder over the base.

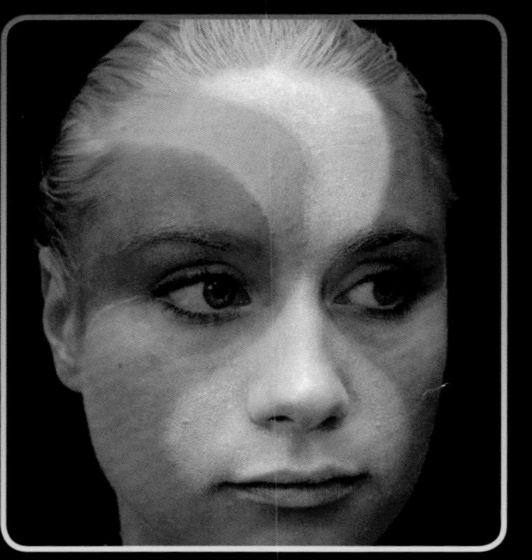

3 Add large sections of mauve and teal across the eyes and forehead to continue the swirl design.

4 Use a number four round brush to apply purple around the edge of the design. Drag blend this out with the tip of the brush. Go round the edges again with a fine line of black – this gives the design incredible contrast.

5 Edge the muzzle in black using a scallop shape outline for a more feminine cat. Using a dry brush, drag the whisker lines in (I learnt this trick from Christina Davison). Paint the lips pink, add glitter and then add some creative lines and accent dots to

be done in six or seven minutes.

1 Working in the opposite direction to the Abstract Cat, outline your design lightly in white and then fill in the swirl across the centre of the face and muzzle in mango. Create the base of the eye design with teal, mauve and copper.

2 Outline the design quite heavily in purple. Don't forget to line the eyes too.

3 Add some large mauve and purple triangular sections on the opposite cheek to the main design. Apply some topaz gem powder to the muzzle.

4 Edge the design in black and paint on a scallop-shaped muzzle with a black tipped nose. Use the black to create a few tiger stripes radiating from the focal point between the eyes up into the hairline. Paint the bottom lip

Ian had the lenses for this design and I immediately knew the red eyes would look really good with a green face and a wild look!

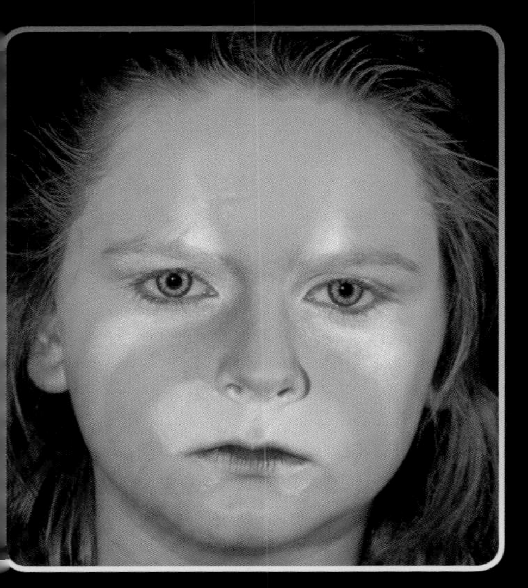

1 Using a dry sponge technique to create an airbrush effect, apply the base. I used mango for the nose, white for the muzzle and eyes, and lime green on the forehead and cheeks.

2 Apply a shade of dark green between the eyes for the shadowing. In the same colour sponge a few triangular segments around the face.

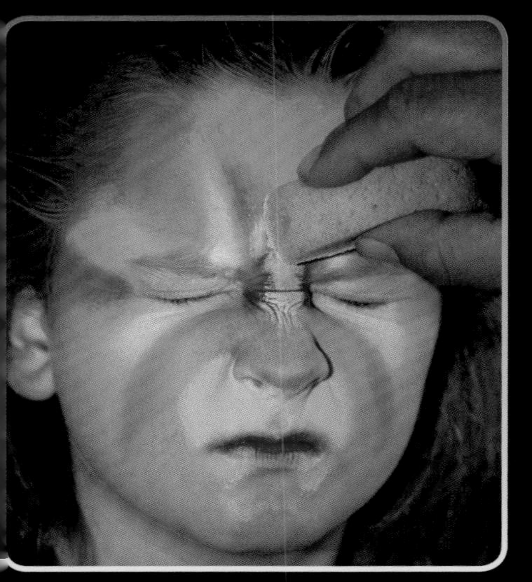

3 Whilst your model scrunches up their face, sponge white between the eyes to create wrinkles.

4 Paint the eyelids in black and start the tiger stripes on the forehead.

Model: Ian

5 Continue the stripes, making sure they all flow to the focal point between the eyes. Still with the black, emphasise the wrinkles, paint on a muzzle with whisker holes and paint the lips and tip of the nose. Add a few irregular shaped dots between the stripes in places. Finish with a pair of white fangs.

Tropical Tiger

Keeping it simple is always good. Here I tried something a bit different with the lines and it worked. Even the wisps on the outer muzzle are simple but effective.

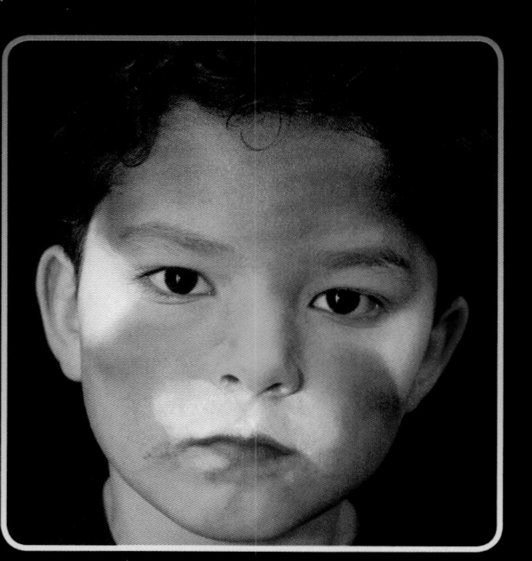

1 Sponge on the base. Use lime in the centre, green and blue metallic paints for the forehead and cheeks and white around the mouth and on the top of the cheekbones.

2 Paint the eyelids black, giving them a pyramid shape leading out to a point. Start the tiger stripes with black angular eyebrows. These will create the starting point for the flow of your design.

3 Add more black lines flowing towards the focal point between the eyes. Paint the end of the nose with a teal colour.

4 Outline the teal nose in black and create the shape of the muzzle. I have added downward strokes to the muzzle to give it a furry feel. Finish the stripes on the face, flowing from

w teal accent dots in the stripes to complement the nose and add black lips and white fangs

Fantasy KISS Tiger

Cat designs can easily be mixed with other styles. This is a classic example where tiger features are combined with KISS style make-up to create one cool design.

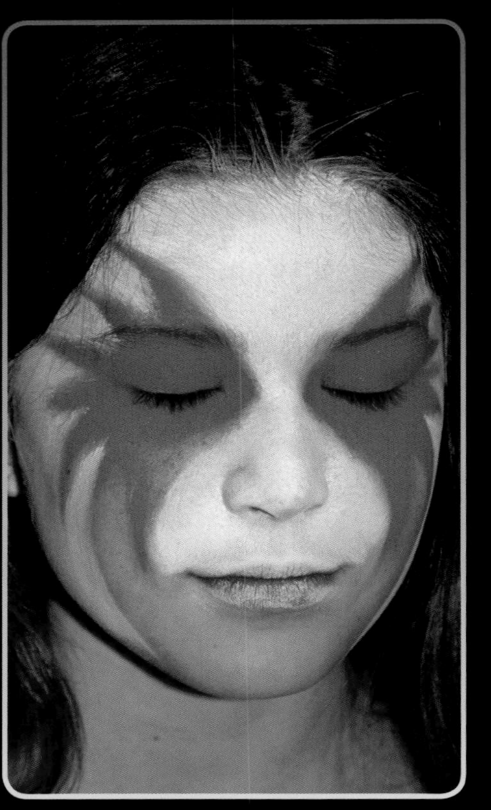

1 Sponge on a white base around the outside of the face and create a muzzle shape round the nose and mouth. In pink, sponge KISS style wings over the eyes and cheeks.

2 Using a large smoothie blender, cover the painted area with shimmer powder. With a number four round brush, outline the eye design with dark purple. I like to use black around the mouth area and for the tip of the nose.

3 Continue to outline the muzzle shape and whisker holes in black. Then edge the tips of the eye design with some bright orange and use some teal to add accent dots. I finished this face with some tiger stripes on the forehead and pink on the

Flaming Tiger

Even in solid black, flames can be very graceful. Make sure the flames flow with the face and overall design.

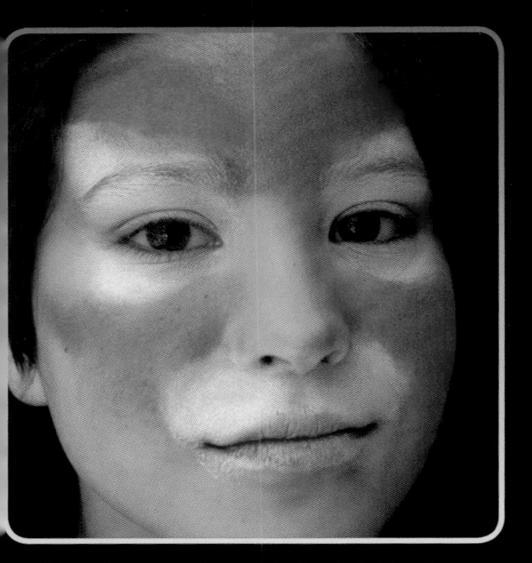

1 Start with the same base as for the Basic Tiger (see p12). Sponge white around the mouth and eyes, mango between and below the eyes and orange to shape the face around the cheeks and forehead.

2 Use a number four round brush to paint dramatic stripes around the eyes. Paint these with flame-like endings across the forehead, spreading out from the focal point between the eyes.

3 Add the nose and a slightly scallop-shaped muzzle in black.

4 Still with black, underline the eyes. Create more flame-like stripes pointing to the focal point and following the cheekbones and shape of the face as well as the shape of the muzzle.

e fangs and red lips

Coming up with something on the spur of the moment can sometimes be pretty frustrating. But when I looked at Annie, this face was all I could see.

1 With a sponge, apply the white base of the muzzle and wing shapes over the forehead and cheeks.

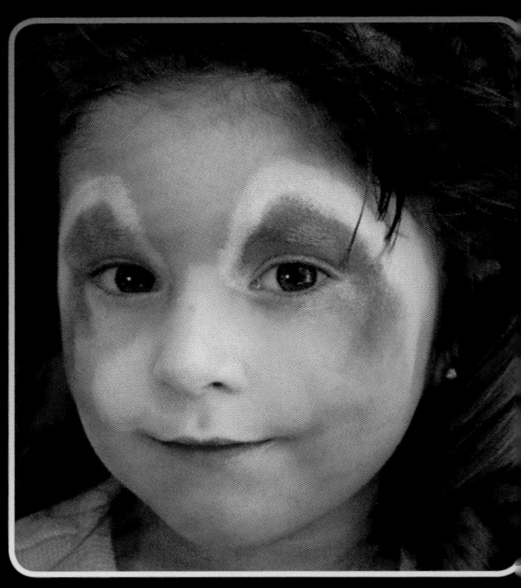

2 Apply pink above the eyes and down the sides onto the cheekbones, staying inside the white base.

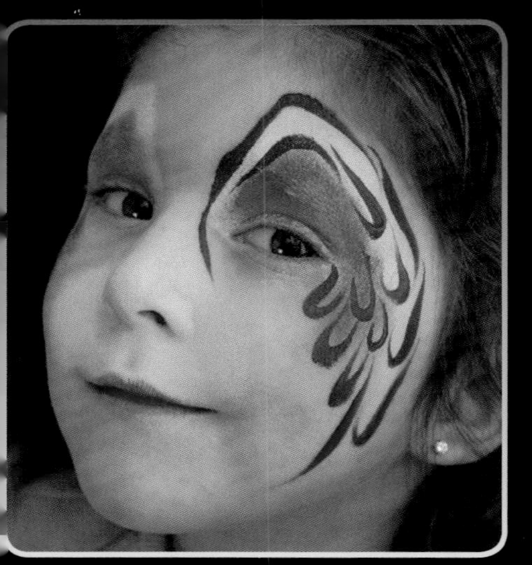

3 With dark purple on a number four brush, paint soft 'u-turns' as explained on the Basic Spotted Cat design (see p10) to create wings that follow the shape of the face.

4 Continue with the dark purple to add some cat-like dots under the eyes. Paint the nose pink and outline with black. Still in black, line the eyes and create a muzzle.

Model: Annie

5 **Finish by outlining the lips in black, filling in with pink and highlighting with glitter.**

Whiskers

When I first painted Korinna as a tiger, she asked if she'd get to have whiskers. Strangely, there on my desk were scissors and copy paper...go figure!

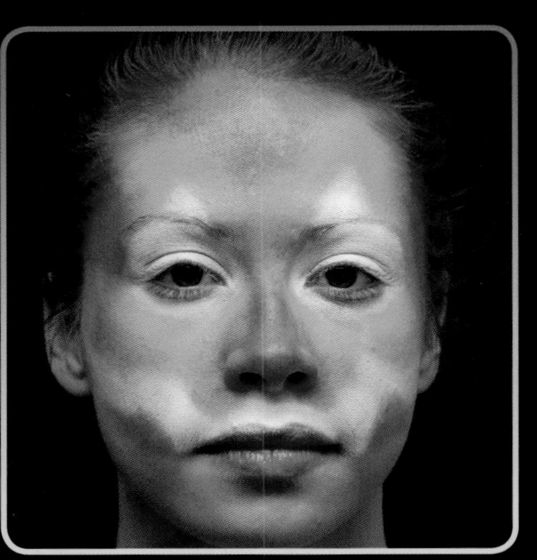

1 Start with the same base as for the Basic Tiger (see p12). Sponge white around the mouth and eyes, mango between and below the eyes and orange to shape the face around the cheeks and forehead. This time, take the white out a bit further across the cheeks.

2 With black on a number four brush, start to apply the lines around the eyes.

3 Cover the centre of the forehead and cheeks with lines radiating from the focal point between the eyes. Add a black muzzle and pink nose.

4 Cut thin strips of white paper for the whiskers.

to apply the whisk

I immediately noticed the red in Katheryn's hair, so I used this as my starting point and used colours that would complement it.

1 Sponge the base shapes for the design around the eye and above the mouth in sparkle yellow and sparkle copper. Line the eye in dark purple.

2 Edge the design with the dark purple using a number four round brush. Then lace the edges with black and drag blend into the purple. Use black to create the outline of the muzzle and nose.

3 Add some cat stripes and some more abstract lines around the eyes with black. Finish the muzzle with whisker hole lines.

4 You could stop here, but once I had started, painting just the face didn't seem enough, so I continued the design on to one shoulder. Lay the same base of sparkle yellow and

5 With the rest of your black lines get creative and make sure that everything flows. Add some gold highlight dots. Finally, I

Copper Cat

I chose the sparkle copper base of this cat to match Bethanie's amazing red hair and the green complementary colour to contrast with it!

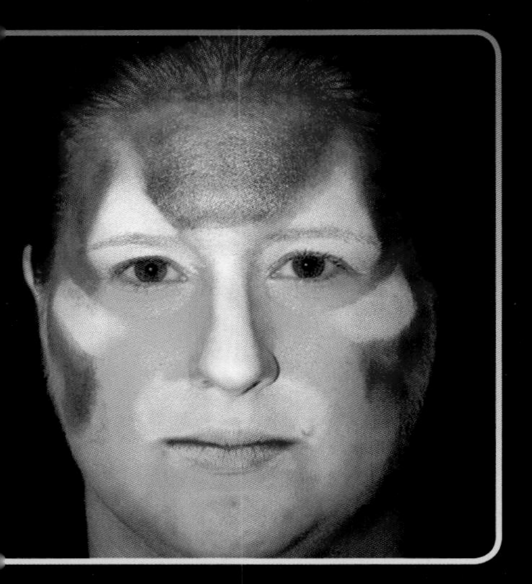

Sponge on the base. I used white above the eyes, on the top of the cheekbones, around the mouth for the muzzle, this time, all the way down the centre of the nose. Sponge arkle copper on the forehead and around the sides of the e and then sparkle yellow in the centre.

2 With black on a number four round brush, line the eyes, paint a muzzle and start the tiger stripes. This time, I went for a butterfly wing shape on the cheeks, but still radiating from the focal point between the eyes. I thought I'd try lining the sides of the nose just to see – as always, these designs are spur of the moment creations.

Continue the line work and add a few dots either side of the nose.

4 I felt there was something lacking, so I added a few more dots around the muzzle, some extra lines around the eyes and some sparkle copper lip colour.

Model: Bethanie

5 Finally add some bright green just under the eyes and some yellow highlight dots to finish. Bethanie then let down her hair for a wild look!

Fantasy Cat Gallery

Model: Mary.

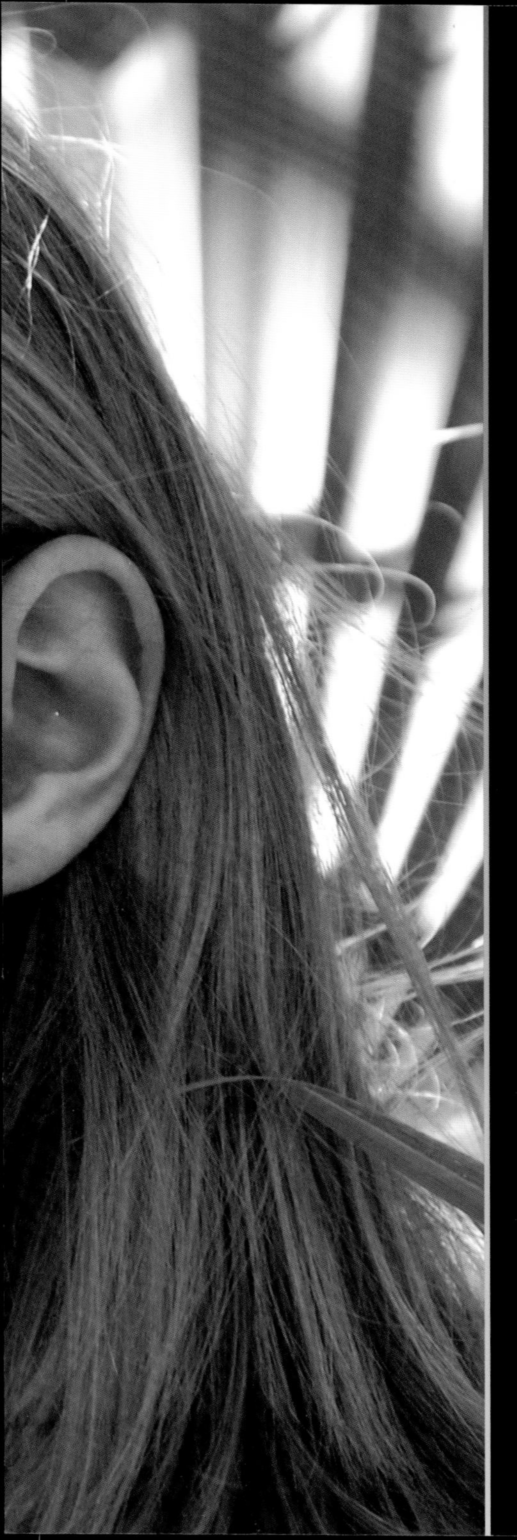

Model: Olivia.

Model: Tashina.

Mark Reid Fantasy

Model: (left) Destiny painted by Mark Reid, (right) painted by Christina Davison on Tiana Tong.

Model: Mya.

Model: Tiana.